Like a Bird With a Thousand Wings

Saint Julian Press

Poetry

Praise for LIKE A BIRD WITH A THOUSAND WINGS

In a tyrannical, divided, and fearful time, we are gifted with travel in a state of grace and awe in Melissa Studdard's exquisite multi-genre book *Like a Bird with a Thousand Wings*. Her poetry brings together the ancient and contemporary, East and West, the individual and collaborative, and the arts of poetry, music, translation, and painting. Studdard writes in response to Christopher Theofanidis's composition, *The Conference of Birds*, a musical interpretation of the allegorical poem by the ancient Persian poet Attãr, translated by Sholeh Wolpé. There are echoes here of the music-driven language of the ecstatic mystical poet, Gerard Manley Hopkins: "Your wings / flame to flight—arching and lifting, / wimpling and waving. Soon / … you are one again with the wonder / of dappled light." Studdard's poems transport us to the visionary world where art generates art and in which we communicate intimately with each other across the millennia and languages and the vast Earth's geography. To read this book is to soar with a conference of birds toward God's mystery, "sun-up towards light / and a thump under the chest answers yes and yes and yes and yes."

— Aliki Barnstone
Author of *Dwelling*, *Bright Body*
and *Dear God, Dear Dr. Heartbreak*

Like a Bird with a Thousand Wings is a cross-cultural dialogue and a significant literary and artistic contribution. It blends poetry and music to unsurpassed effect to tell the tale of perseverance, survival, and search for knowledge. The book is inspired by Attar's poetical masterpiece, *The Conference of the Birds*, the story of a journey that starts with the birds' search for the legendary Simorgh only to end with the discovery of self. This mystifying book gives the reader an unsatiating desire to rediscover it anew on repeated readings.

— Sheema Kalbasi
Author of *Echoes in Exile*
Editor of *Seven Valleys of Love* and
The Poetry of Iranian Women

There is a creative murmuration at work in this gorgeous collaboration which flows out of an intuitive and synergistic whole. The rapturous power within Studdard's poems draws as deeply from the Divine as from the exquisite compositions of Theofanidis. These fresh, original poems stun the senses and the ecstatic pulse of the reader, raising the whole of this artistic union to new heights. Theofanidis's arrangements act as an incandescent current allowing the arc of narrative to take flight through Attar's seven valleys. These compositions fuse elements of humankind's struggle from the denser quest for knowledge to the ecstatic joy of wonderment told exquisitely through the dynamic strings and melodic agency of the Argus quartet. Studdard's poems turn this course through breath and shadow to place us directly in the line of this union's collective truth. If everyone understood the authentic meaning of these verses and the empowerment of infinite existence, this purgatory we call earth would transform at once to heaven. Not the heaven of rewards and punishments, not the Garden of Eden but the song which created the apple. "Let us consume/the shimmering, false distance/between yourself and everything you see/so that you may be a conduit/to bring these warm, pulsing/wonders to the world/still breathing and throbbing/with life." Let us witness our great thousand-winged bird, so stunningly embodied through the sublime art of Elisa Vendramin, then witness our wings disappear.

— Lois P. Jones
Author of *Night Ladder*

A mosaic of beauty, *Like a Bird with a Thousand Wings* weaves together the brilliant poems of Melissa Studdard and the artistic genius of composer Christopher Theofanidis, along with artwork by Elisa Vendramin, creating a perfect combination of splendor. Studdard, who is one of the best American poets writing today, creates poems that exist with both an exquisiteness and passion, poems where love is birdsong and breath; her work, so gifted, skillful, and tender you want to give it / to everyone you meet. Combined with the striking elegance Theofanidis's musical compositions on the page, the collaboration brings to mind visions of birds on a wire and birds in flight. I wasn't prepared for so much beauty in one book, how the arts can intertwine and bring all of us in. Reading this book, I found my own heart taking part in this magnificent flight of minds — "an arch of wing lifts sun-up towards light, / and a thump under the chest answers, Yes and yes and yes and yes." *Like a Bird with a Thousand Wings* is a gift to the world like none I have ever seen and a collaboration we are lucky to hold in our hands.

— Kelli Russell Agodon
Author of *Hourglass Museum*, *Small Knots*
and *Letters from the Emily Dickinson Room*

LIKE A BIRD WITH A THOUSAND WINGS

Poems

by

Melissa Studdard

Written to Accompany Christopher Theofanidis'
The Conference of the Birds for String Quartet
which Traces the Metaphoric Journey
of Attār's *The Conference of the Birds*

SAINT JULIAN PRESS
HOUSTON

Published by
SAINT JULIAN PRESS, Inc.
2053 Cortlandt, Suite 200
Houston, Texas 77008

www.saintjulianpress.com

LIKE A BIRD WITH A THOUSAND WINGS
COPYRIGHT © 2020
TWO THOUSAND AND TWENTY
By Melissa Studdard

ISBN-13: 978-1-7330233-1-3
ISBN: 1-7330233-1-3
Library of Congress Control Number: 2020931951

Musical excerpts from Christopher Theofanidis' *The Conference of the Birds*
Copyright © 2017 by Christopher Theofanidis (ASCAP). All Rights Reserved. Used by Permission.
Sole Agent: Bill Holab Music

Cover & Interior Art
SIMURGH by Elisa Vendramin
Copyright © 2019

Melissa Studdard's portrait by Alexis Rhone Fancher
Christopher Theofanidis' portrait by Matthew Fried

FOR OUR RESPECTIVE CHILDREN, ROSALIND AND ISABELLA
AND FOR SEEKERS AND PEACEMAKERS EVERYWHERE

PREFACE

In the complex world dynamics of today, it feels more important than ever to remind ourselves that cultural heritage outlasts and outweighs political climates and that art is one of the vehicles through which we can transcend our differences to find our common humanity. Tracing back to the most ancient literary texts, we see that although the details of our lives and environments change with the times, the basic fears and aspirations of humankind remain the same. We look to the arts to show us what we most need to see about ourselves—that we are in the end, all of us, a human family.

The Conference of the Birds, the 12th Century Sufi allegorical poem by Persian poet Attār, deals with these universal themes. *Conference* tells the story of the seeker's journey towards God, towards the evolution of self through wisdom, love, openness, and connection. In it, all the birds of the world convene and determine that they need a ruler. Such a leader is known in the form of the mythic and divine bird, Simorgh, who resides in a distant land. The journey to this faraway place leads the birds through seven valleys of understanding, the first of which requires them to cast off all the preconceived ideas and dogma in their thinking, and the final of which requires annihilation of the self in order to attain complete communion with the divine.

Beginning with the discord and lack of purpose of the birds and culminating in the discovery that they are all individually and together Simorgh, *The Conference of the Birds* is a timeless model of transforming confusion and lack of unity into the realization of harmony and purpose.

Christopher's piece, released in 2018, traces the metaphoric journey of the birds in seven short character pieces, each lasting between one and three minutes, and each focusing on a highly defined musical personality evoked by the corresponding valley. Much of the string writing is inspired by the flocking movement of birds; that is, there is a 'group logic'—a kind of unity of movement and purpose in which all the parts are highly interdependent.

In the fall of 2019, the Argus Quartet, who were performing *The Conference of the Birds*, contacted Christopher to discuss the possibility of reciting poems in performance between the musical pieces, and Christopher recommended that Melissa write the text. The resulting poems, which became *Like a Bird with a Thousand Wings*, respond most intimately to Christopher's musical interpretation of the valleys but were written, as well, in consultation with Sholeh Wolpé's contemporary translation of Attãr's *The Conference of the Birds* (W.W. Norton & Co).

Rather than retelling Attãr's allegory, Melissa's poems intend to provide imagery and language to illuminate and accentuate specific qualities of the sound journey Christopher has created in response to Attãr. In order to tease out Attãr's narrative sequence, Melissa has woven mini summaries, as well as quotes from various translations, through the text.

It is our hope that by uniting the artistic disciplines of poetry, composition, visual art, and performance, Attãr's vital allegory will be brought further to life on the stage and in other artistic mediums.

Melissa Studdard & Christopher Theofanidis
January 19, 2020
Manasota Key, Florida

If Simorgh unveils its face to you, you will find
that all the birds, be they thirty or forty or more,
are but the shadows cast by that unveiling.
What shadow is ever separated from its maker?
Do you see?
The shadow and its maker are one and the same,
so get over surfaces and delve into mysteries.

Attãr
Translated by Sholeh Wolpé

CONTENTS

PROLOGUE 1

WHEN THE BIRDSONG RINGS HUMAN   2

VALLEY OF THE QUEST   3

THERE'S A BRIGHTNESS FOLDED INTO EVERY BIRD   7

VALLEY OF LOVE   9

LIKE SHINING FROM SHOOK FOIL   13

VALLEY OF KNOWLEDGE   15

LIKE A DIAMOND WITH NO ANSWER

OR A KEY THAT OPENS ALL THE LOCKS   19

VALLEY OF DETACHMENT   21

BUT WHO WILL HEAR YOU

FROM SO FAR ACROSS THE SKY   25

VALLEY OF UNITY 27

THE BODY IS THE SONG 31

VALLEY OF WONDERMENT 33

LEAVE ALL THE WINDOWS OF YOUR SOUL CRACKED OPEN 37

VALLEY OF POVERTY AND ANNIHILATION 39

WHEN THE BIRDSONG RINGS DIVINE 43

JOURNEY'S END 45

BLESSED AIGRETTE: WE ARE ALL

A BIRD NAMED "SIMORGH" 48

ACKNOWLEDGEMENTS

NOTES

ABOUT THE ARTISTS

Like a Bird with a Thousand Wings

PROLOGUE

Led by the hoopoe bird, the birds of the world form a flock to seek their king, the divine and mysterious Simorgh, who resides at the other end of the earth.

WHEN THE BIRDSONG RINGS HUMAN

the hoopoe bird forgets its tongue, like a time traveler
accidentally leaving a glove in a year that hasn't
happened. The tongue wanders strange gray
streets, its sour and sweet buds lit up
with the hoopoe's hunger, glowing like a jellyfish
in the rain. Now the tongue knows no house can
promise safety. Not the sheath of mouth. Not even
the body, which laughs at the body of time, stretched
like a poolside lizard across dimensions. The tongue
bellows for the hoopoe across the green. The
hoopoe hears what he thinks is an echo—not
blazing, but persistent, ever-present, a little fuzzy,
like a radio that's not coming in well or the hum
and buzz of the streetlamps and telephone wires
he knew in that other world. Everything
the bird means to say turns ancient at the root
and falls off. Because God is not a clock, nor a sundial,
reaching forward with narrow arms. God is a million
tiny pieces, like glitter, or destiny, breaking flesh
into astonishment, breaking pain into daggers of light.

VALLEY OF THE QUEST

Stand empty-handed,
and the cleansing of your heart begins.

Purge your heart of its own traits,
and the virtues of the divine will reflect in it.

Attãr
Translated by Sholeh Wolpé

VALLEY OF THE QUEST

Through a series of trials that strip them of dogma, preconceived notions, and fear, the birds are emptied of themselves and filled with purpose and possibility.

Commissioned by the Howard Hanson Institute for American Music of the Eastman School of Music at the University of Rochester for the Ying Quartet

The Conference of the Birds
(2017)

Christopher Theofanidis

Quarter note trills and harmonics in this mvt. should be played with some length.

I. Valley of Quest
Gioioso ♩ = 144

THERE'S A BRIGHTNESS FOLDED INTO EVERY BIRD

but the bird doesn't know it. The bird is thirty birds who soared
out of dreaming to invent sky, thirty birds flying in the formation

of a bird. God tells them, *Open, O moon-beak O silver-black O sliver
of luck*, and the bird says, *Break me until I'm whole*. God says, *Empty,*

and the bird spills a splendor of jewels from their thirty beaks into
the valley. *Don't think I'm a diamond*, God says, *Find me*, and hands

the bird a map back to the inside of their own bone, then disappears.
But the bird doesn't understand the quest(ion). Thirty birds split

into a thousand that search under everything—stone, fabric,
sun-face, gold—until they find no God. Now the beak yells, *Take*

me; I have no reason, and an arch of wing lifts sun-up towards light,
and a thump under the chest answers, *Yes* and *yes* and *yes* and *yes*.

VALLEY OF LOVE

In this valley, love is fire, mind is smoke.
When love arrives, reason flees.

Attār
Translated by Sholeh Wolpé

VALLEY OF LOVE

The birds traverse the metaphoric flames of love, burning off all reason.

LIKE SHINING FROM SHOOK FOIL

You're in a valley
and flying. You know a thousand
other words for *behold*,
a hundred thousand for *dapple-dale*.
Below, a century begins and ends
and no one remembers the details.
You mistake a sheep's sigh
for sadness and fall in love
with the sound of cloud emanating from lungs.
You mistake a horse's whinny for winter
and stop for a hundred years to build and stoke
a fire to keep the horse warm.
You are a bird,
no,
thirty birds,
no,
a thousand. Your wings
flame to flight—arching and lifting,
wimpling and waving. Soon
the movement lifts you
and you are one again with the wonder
of dappled light. You coax
honey from a topaz stone
and feed it to a cloud. Love will
break you
into the gift of your life.
Give it
to everyone you meet.
There's no right or wrong here,
only warmth
rushing from you
like embers to the wind—

VALLEY OF KNOWLEDGE

If you do not see the beloved's face
get up! What are you waiting for?
Go look for it!

Attãr
Translated by Sholeh Wolpé

VALLEY OF KNOWLEDGE

Entering mystery, the birds release worldly knowledge in favor of wisdom.

III. Valley of Knowledge
Inquieto ♩ = 144

LIKE A DIAMOND WITH NO ANSWER, OR A KEY THAT OPENS ALL THE LOCKS

And who has not at one point
scraped the bottom of self
to invent a new self? Who has not
dropped the diamond to pick up
a ruby, dropped the ruby to
scoop a peridot from a pea pod?
One bird tosses another a gold-set pearl
of wisdom. The bird drops it and another
picks it up, rolls it across a talon
and into a beak, tosses it up up
like a golden bracelet
twisting on its chains. One link
is the hoopoe bird
wending into ignorance,
one is the parrot, forgetting
what to say, one is the peacock,
fanning out
unseeing eyes. Everything they
thought they knew
turns tarnished at the tip
and drifts off. Who will answer
the question? Who will
answer the question
no one asked? *Look at me*, God says,
holding up a key,
and the bird spills
a schoolhouse
of jewels
from their mouth.

VALLEY OF DETACHMENT

If everything is erased, from the moonfish to the moon,
here, it's as if an ant has injured its leg in a well.
If both worlds perish in a flash,
it's as if a grain of sand has gone missing.

Attãr
Translated by Sholeh Wolpé

VALLEY OF DETACHMENT

Reality as they knew it no longer makes sense. What seemed to matter no longer matters. The birds let go of all attachments and desires.

IV. Valley of Detachment

24

BUT WHO WILL HEAR YOU
FROM SO FAR ACROSS THE SKY?

Self is the place
we keep getting sewn back into.
We fly away.
It sews us back. We tear
the fabric, here comes the needle.
Try falling down the well
of yourself. Little clicks
along the way.
Little bright spots
before the dark.
It happens more slowly
than you previously
thought.
Dismantle your bones
and build a new God.

VALLEY OF UNITY

Everything here is outside of time,
outside of measurements,
so forget about the beginning,
forget about the end.

Attãr
Translated by Sholeh Wolpé

VALLEY OF UNITY

The birds discover that every part of being is interconnected, and they are a divine whole.

V. Valley of Unity
Grazioso ♩ = 84

Each of these (dotted) half/quarter groupings should be felt in one connected gesture; grace notes should be accented

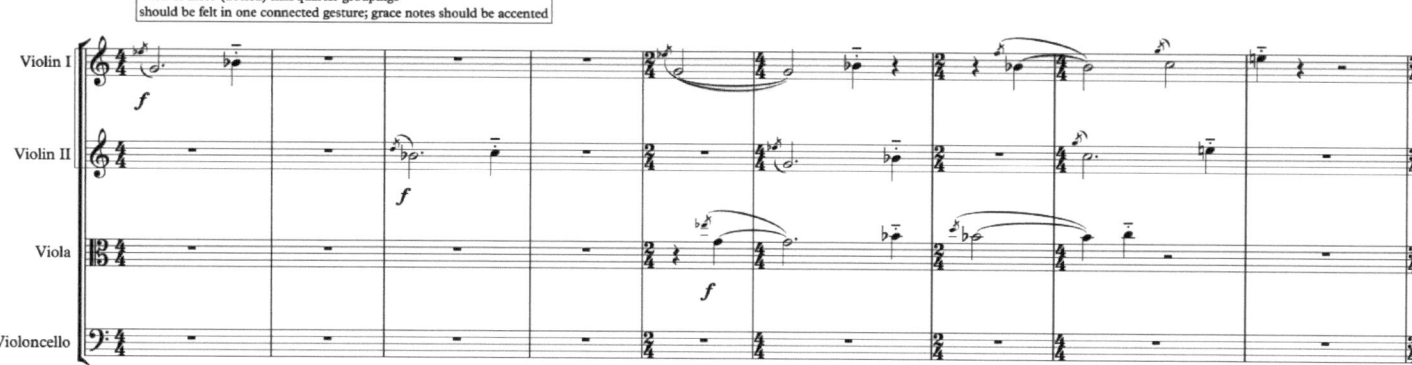

THE BODY IS THE SONG

Now, God has filled you with singing birds.
God has filled the singing birds with you.
A ruby-throated chirp
lifts from an emerald-lined
limb. An orange-throated warble
wafts through a larimar sky. Then,
all the birds turn towards the center of you,
quiet. Through gauzy, windblown curtains
you see flashes of light, dancing
rays spun round
a spinning child, beneath the blooming
greengage plums, beneath
the drift of dandelion puff.
You are the child, and the child is you.
Who is the birdsong? Who
is the emerald?
Who is the light? Consume
the shimmering, false distance
between yourself and everything you see
so that you may be a conduit
to bring these warm, pulsing
wonders to the world
still breathing and throbbing
with life.

VALLEY OF WONDERMENT

And if you stamp the seal of oneness on your soul,
you'll drift even further in your lostness.

Attãr
Translated by Sholeh Wolpé

VALLEY OF WONDERMENT

Entering the great paradox of divine awe, the birds discover they know nothing. They are both lost and found, both empty and full.

VI. Valley of Wonderment
Allegro ♩ = 90

LEAVE ALL THE WINDOWS OF YOUR SOUL CRACKED OPEN

Stretch your wings wide as God's first breath.

From tip to tip there is no time. Just
the rumbling of a tune in your makeshift

beak, and bright sky galloping through

the hollow of bone. Bucket of air, spine
built from light, bird full of flutters

and drafts—you speak mountain stream,

laurel leaf, rolling cloud—the dialect
of flight. The world drifts like a current

inside you—rivers, trees, and hills, feathers,

wings, and light, the start and end of time
rowing through blood's currents, sailing

inside the freedom of mind, now split

open by a whirlwind of koan, pushed
like air through sky's vast lung.

VALLEY OF POVERTY AND ANNIHILATION

When a lute and common kindling
meet in fire, they both burn
for they are made of the same wood.
But their attributes are not the same.

Attãr
Translated by Sholeh Wolpé

VALLEY OF POVERTY AND ANNIHILATION

The birds now fly outside of time, losing their ego selves in the void of completion. They are nothing; they are everything; they are absorbed into the whole.

VII. Valley of Poverty and Annihiliation
Cantabile ♩ = 66

WHEN THE BIRDSONG RINGS DIVINE

shining brighter than
a silverfish
that has come apart in the hands, every bird
builds its own God.

Every bird
leaves itself in the valley's
whorl,
builds it world
from fish bones
and limestone.

To be and not to be, that
is the answer.

Because your body
is the instrument
of longing.

Did you play it
or did it play you?

Toss your instrument
to the wind.

JOURNEY'S END

When they looked at Simorgh,
Simorgh was where they themselves stood.
And when they looked at themselves,
they saw Simorgh standing there too.
And when they looked at both,
both were one and the same in every way.

Attãr
Translated by Sholeh Wolpé

JOURNEY'S END

Out of the thousands of birds that began the journey, thirty birds make it to the end, finally finding the great Simorgh.

BLESSED AIGRETTE: WE ARE ALL A BIRD NAMED "SIMORGH"

When the birdsong rings human
there's a brightness folded into every bird
like shining from shook foil,
like a diamond with no answer,
or a key that opens all the locks,
but who will
hear you from so far across the sky?
The body is the song,
So leave the windows
of your soul cracked open
when the birdsong rings divine.

ACKNOWLEDGMENTS

With gratitude to the Argus String Quartet
and The Hermitage Artist Retreat
for making the collaboration possible

and gratitude to Sholeh Wolpé
for quotes and inspiration from her
new translation of *The Conference of the Birds*

and with humble and gracious gratitude to
the original commissioners of the piece:
the Howard Hanson Institute for American Music
of the Eastman School of Music
at the University of Rochester
for the Ying Quartet.

With gratitude to Italian artist Elisa Vendramin
whose work adorns the cover and interior pages of
Like A Bird With A Thousand Wings.

And finally, with gratitude to publisher Ron Starbuck for
his infinite wisdom, patience, and graciousness.

NOTES

1. Epigraph: "Parable of the King's Mirror" from *The Conference of the Birds* by Attãr, translated by Sholeh Wolpé. W. W. Norton & Company; (April 17, 2019). ISBN–13: 978-0393355543
2. All Translations: from *The Conference of the Birds* by Attãr, translated by Sholeh Wolpé. W. W. Norton & Company; (April 17, 2019). ISBN–13: 978-0393355543
3. "When the birdsong rings divine" is an adaptation of my poem "When the birdsong rings human," originally published in *New England Review*, and is also part of my *Philomela's Tongue* manuscript-in-progress.
4. The title "Like Shining from Shook Foil" is a phrase from Gerard Manley Hopkins' "God's Grandeur."
5. "The Valley of Unity: The Body Is the Song" contains several lines adapted from my poem, "Poet," originally published in the *Hip Poetry 2012* anthology.
6. "Leave All the Windows of your Soul Cracked Open" is an adaptation of my poem "You Were a Bird; You are a Sea," from the book *I Ate the Cosmos for Breakfast*.
7. "To be and not to be" alludes to Hamlet's "to be or not to be."
8. Simorgh, means thirty (*si*) birds *(morgh)*.
9. Blessed aigrette is a form I created for this chapbook. It takes the titles of the all the previous poems in the book, in order, and makes a new poem from them. I realized after I'd written it that it shares characteristics with another form, the heroic crown of sonnets. The heroic crown strings together fifteen sonnets, with the final poem using the first lines of the previous poems to create a new poem. I wanted to honor Iranian culture, as well as the birds, in naming this new form, so I chose "aigrette" in place of "crown." An aigrette is a spray of feathers or jewels that adorns a headdress, and which is meant to resemble the tufted crest of an egret. Though I'm not a fan of taking feathers from birds, I love the idea of a spray of jewels to resemble the crest. The Iranian National Jewels collection features many gorgeous, jeweled aigrettes. And finally, in changing "heroic" to "blessed," I wanted to highlight the spiritual nature of the birds' journey.

ABOUT THE ARTISTS

MELISSA STUDDARD is the author of four previous books, including the poetry collection *I Ate the Cosmos for Breakfast*. Her short writings have appeared or been featured in a wide variety of periodicals, such as *The New York Times*, POETRY, *Psychology Today*, *The Guardian*, and the Academy of American Poets' Poem-a-Day Series. Her work has been listed among Amazon's most gifted books and has garnered awards such as *The Penn Review* Poetry Prize, the International Book Award, and the REELpoetry Audience Choice Award. Website: https://melissastuddard.com

CHRISTOPHER THEOFANIDIS' music has been performed by many of the world's leading performing arts organizations, from the London Symphony and New York Philharmonic to the San Francisco Opera and the American Ballet Theatre. He is a two-time Grammy nominee, and his work, *Rainbow Body*, is one of the most performed works of the new era, having been performed by over 150 orchestras worldwide. Mr. Theofanidis is currently on the faculty at Yale University and the Aspen Music Festival. Website: https://www.theofanidismusic.com

ELISA VENDRAMIN is an Italian illustrator based between Reykjavik, Iceland and Trieste, Italy. She plays with abstraction in digital collages, exploring the delicate balance between full and empty, aiming to capture those atmospheres that are often hard to describe by words or by figurative illustration. She graduated with a Master's in Communication Design, from Central Saint Martins College of Art and Design, London. Her artwork has been featured in cultural projects across Europe and Asia, most recently for the MuseumsQuartier, in Vienna, Austria, one of the largest districts for contemporary art and culture in the world. Website: http://www.elisavendramin.co.uk

Type Setting:

GARAMOND 11 — Garamond 11
PERPETUA TILTING MT 13
PERPETUA TILTING MT 12

www.ingramcontent.com/pod-product-compliance
Lightning Source LLC
Chambersburg PA
CBHW040629200426

43193CB00061B/53